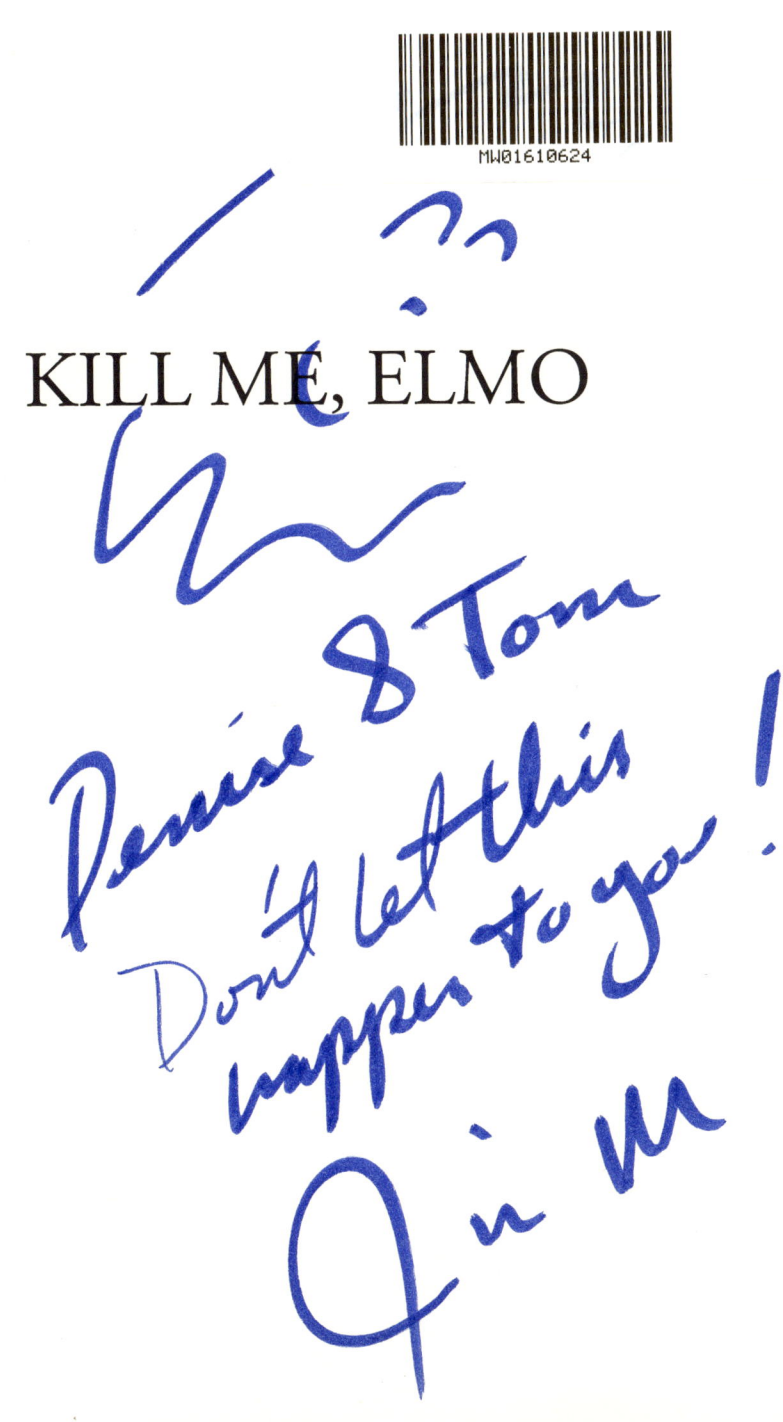

KILL ME, ELMO

Denise & Tom
Don't let this
happen to you!

Jim M

Other books by Jim Mullen:

How to Lose Money—In Your Spare Time—at Home!

Now in Paperback!

My First Wedding: A Planner for Modern Couples

Baby's First Tattoo: A Memory Book for Modern Parents

It Takes A Village Idiot: Complicating the Simple Life

and

Paisley Goes with Nothing
   by Hal Rubenstein with Jim Mullen

Anthologies:

May Contain Nuts

101 Damnations

KILL ME, ELMO

The
Holiday
Depression
Fun Book

Jim Mullen

NEWS INK INC.

NEWS INK INC.
www.newsinkinc.com

Copyright © 2012 by Jim Mullen

This is a work of fiction.
Most of the characters appearing in this work are fictitious.
Any resemblance to real persons, living or dead,
who are not related to me in some way, is purely coincidental.

Parts of this book first appeared in "The Village Idiot,"
a newspaper column syndicated by
Newspaper Enterprise Association, a division of United Media.

Designed by Terry Bradshaw

www.jimmullenbooks.com
ISBN 978-1-4792632-5-7

KILL ME, ELMO

Mission: Improbable

I stuffed an extra bottle of pepper spray in my coat pocket and patted myself down to make sure I hadn't forgotten to bring my brass knuckles, numchucks, and a blackjack. I had filed my fingernails to sharp points and I was wearing steel-toed boots and a kevlar vest. Was I totally prepared for this mission? Would I make it back in one piece? I considered adding football pads but they might cause more problems than they solved in a tight space. I did go with wrist guards and knee braces. I double-checked my pockets and ran through the checklist in my head. Good thing, I almost forgot my shopping list. That would have been a rookie mistake—to go Black Friday shopping without a list. On that path lies certain death.

Full of the Black Friday spirit, I headed off to the mall. It wouldn't be light yet for four hours, the perfect time to scout the place, to check the perimeter, to plan my parking, to take the high ground before the enemy takes the field. Too late! The parking lot is full! And no cars are leaving. There are cars in front of me and behind me. None of them can park and none of them can leave. If I stop for even half a second the horns start to blow followed by insults shouted out open car windows. Each time I think I have found a space, it turns out to be just a very small car. How, I wonder, are they ever going to get a giant wall-size TV in that dinky little thing? Why, oh, why didn't I think to bring a tank? I'd just park it on top of that little tin can. It took me an hour to find a spot in Overflow Parking Lot Number 3 and then I had to wait for the shuttle bus to get me back to the mall.

By the time I got there it looked like New Year's Eve in Times Square. I supposed I could come back the next week, but then I'd be taking the chance that all the good stuff would be gone. Everyone knows the only time the stores are full of merchandise is the day after Thanksgiving. After that, they are totally empty, stripped down to the bare walls. When I thought of the faces of all the disappointed children who would get nothing if I didn't get inside and buy myself a 60-inch TV for 30 percent off, I had to hold back the tears. I was also planning to spend a few bucks buying crappy trinkets for the kids on my way out, but no TV, no trinkets. Who do they think I am? Santa Claus?

Suddenly, I was filled with the true meaning of Christmas shopping. I reached under my coat and felt for my Taser. I'd blast the grandma pushing the stroller in front of me and in the ensuing panic I'd move to the head of the line. I pressed it into her neck and pulled the trigger. Nothing. I forgot to charge it. It was totally depleted. I'd forgotten how much I must have used it working for a collection agency. You wouldn't believe how many people haven't finished paying for the stuff they bought last Black Friday.

Grandma turned around and bit my trigger finger while alternately kicking me in the groin and punching my face. Grandma turned out to be a he and the stroller just a prop to gain sympathy. It wasn't working. The day hadn't gone the way he planned, either. No one seemed to notice our little dust-up; they were all on their iPhones trying to find deals on newer and better iPhones or squabbling among themselves for a better spot in line. This was getting out of hand. I didn't see any security at all from the store. Then it hit me—all I had to do next year was buy a security guard's uniform. I could walk down the line telling people to calm down and keep order and just walk right up to the front door right as they opened it and walk into the store in front of all the people who had waited all night. After all, isn't that what Christmas is all about?

Why Does Christmas Happen to Good People?

Thanksgiving and Christmas have morphed into something that would be unrecognizable to our not-so-distant ancestors. One of the reasons the Pilgrims left England was that they thought the Church of England was blowing Christmas celebrations all out of proportion by taking *half a day* off. The Puritans who got off the Mayflower in 1620 didn't think Christmas should be celebrated at all. The holiday was banned in Boston from 1639 to 1681. That big thump you just heard was the CEO of Toys 'R' Us fainting. The heads of Hallmark, Walmart, the Cranberry Consortium, the American Turkey Sellers Association and all the domestic airlines have their fingers in their ears and are singing "La, la, la, la, la, la." All of them, and thousands more, are in the business of making you feel guilty if you don't make a long, miserable, and expensive trip to whatever gated, planned, and age-restricted hellhole your parents live in now—The Villages, Sun City, or some other mugger-free community. They don't just want to spoil your Christmas, but your Thanksgiving, Fourth of July, and Shrove Tuesday, too. No matter how awful, stressful, and unpleasant it is, no matter that there is a seventy percent chance that you will end up spending all of your valuable time off stuck in ORD, JFK, or ATL, the holiday hucksters don't want you to remember why you live seven states away from your parents; they want you to do this because of "tradition." A tradition they invented, a tradition they keep exploiting for their benefit, not yours.

It's why you'll never see an ad by the American Stuffing Society showing a drunken mom waving a carving knife over the Thanksgiving turkey hiccoughing, "So, are you bringing your slut girlfriend here for Christmas, too?" or a fed-up dad saying "When are you going to get a real job and stop wasting your life?" It's why holiday advertisements are full of twee Norman Rockwell /

Thomas Kinkade-type memories, scenes of happy family meals with everyone beaming and smiling instead of the bipolar, liquor-fueled food fights that most of these gatherings turn into at some point or another.

The holidays have morphed into a four-month-long shop-athon that starts before Halloween and ends with the Super Bowl, all of it geared to get you to buy everything from ribbon and wrapping paper, from sweet potatoes to guacamole, from cards to gift certificates. Stores will spend millions of ad dollars making you feel guilty and unpatriotic if you're not out there buying trinkets for people you barely know. As if buying things equals love— and UPS, FedEx, car rental companies, airlines, liquor stores, gas stations and malls are depending on you to do your share. If you don't run up a massive holiday credit card debt, the terrorists win. Don't you care enough to spend every dime you have? How much do I love thee? Let me count my credit card debt.

Yet, even after you did everything corporate America told you to do to have the perfect holiday—you shopped, you over-ate, you sent cards—you still got in a tiff with your brother over something that happened fifteen years ago, your sister is pregnant again by a new boyfriend who just hit on your wife, and Dad won't come out of the basement. For all the time and money you spent shopping you'd have been better off taking a cruise in the Caribbean and having a lovely, relaxing, soul-repairing holiday. For the same money you could have flown to Rio or Madrid or Paris, you could have visited the Louvre and walked past Notre Dame at night, but you can't afford to do that now because you wasted all your vacation money so you could hear Aunt Sally repeat the story of her knee replacement for the fifth time and hear once again how well Uncle Bob's sixth grader is doing in soccer. For this you bought a six-hundred-dollar plane ticket? For this you drove fifteen hours?

Most families are like the afternoon soap operas. You can stop following them for five years and pick up right where you left off. So unless your evil twin sister has buried you alive in the back yard or stolen your identity, there's not much new to talk about. There is no point in doing the same thing year after year except for habit.

What if half of all families decided to get together only on odd-numbered years and the other half decided to get together on even-numbered years? Think how much that would cut traffic, how many seats it would free up on the airlines. Why can't we all meet in the Cayman Islands or Oaxaca, instead of Grandpa's house? It's time to start thinking outside the gift-wrapped box and start having fun again.

Are you a bad person because you don't want to spend fifteen hours in a car or an airport to visit Grandma Murphy for fifteen minutes when she hasn't remembered your name for the last six years? Absolutely not. We have let corporate hucksters vandalize our holidays and ruin our peace of mind by turning Holy Days into a never-ending series of pressure-filled Black Fridays and Cyber Mondays, telling us we are unpatriotic if we don't spend money we don't have, if we don't contribute to their bottom line by buying unnecessary, meaningless over-priced tchotchkes.

If you're lucky you won't spend two hours standing at the luggage carousel before you realize that your luggage is never coming out of that little door with the plastic flaps and that you could have left the airport two hours ago, but because you waited they cancelled your rental car reservation and now you're seeing if you can share a $100 cab ride with someone.

If you're lucky your plane won't have to land at a different airport so they can arrest the drunken air-rage passenger who tried to open the emergency doors at 30,000 feet.

If you're lucky you won't be on the crying, screaming baby flight with the parents who pretend the kids aren't theirs.

If you're lucky you'll only be stuck in the traffic jam caused when two texting drivers hit each other head-on for four hours instead of six.

Even if you are lucky, extremely lucky, and none of that comes to pass and you arrive with no delays, and everything went smoothly, and you catch up with your family and you see all the baby pictures and you meet all the new boyfriends and girlfriends and find out how everyone's job (or lack of one) is going, and you've had some laughs and you think, "That was nice, I'm glad I got to see everyone, it's time to go home," you will look at your watch and realize you've only been visiting with your family for three hours and it will be three more long days before you can leave.

That's when it hits you that you've made a terrible, terrible mistake. You feel as if you're in one of those meetings your boss calls all the time that go on way too long and never solve any problems. At first the meeting is productive but after a while it takes all your will power to keep from yawning and falling head first onto the conference table. It hits you that your company is not doing well because we're always in meetings instead of working. The meetings aren't helping the business, they're killing it.

Is the yearly Thanksgiving get-together helping your family or hurting it? The Pilgrims had a nice Thanksgiving without going all the way back to England, didn't they? As a matter of fact, that was one of the things they were giving thanks for, that they didn't *have* to go home. Asking someone to travel any distance to your home on Thanksgiving back then would have been called cruel and unusual punishment. It seems we've come full circle; having to travel on Thanksgiving has once again become cruel and unusual punishment.

Fifty years ago, you could have had twenty close relatives over to your house for Thanksgiving dinner and most of them would have come by foot. Not any more. Now everyone has to drive for hours or fly for hours. During those hours they start to remember why they live six states away, why they took that job with the out-of-town company, why they insisted on going to an out-of-state college.

Long before it's time to leave they'll remember that they don't even like turkey that much.

The Early Bird Gets the Worm. Who Wants a Worm?

Each year the retailers start pushing the holidays on us earlier and earlier. This year the ads started showing up in September. The kids are already talking about what they want to get; parents are already putting up outside lights and decorations and planning big dinners and spending money like there's no tomorrow. Of course, I am talking about the biggest holiday of the year—Halloween.

Who cannot fondly remember their parents spending hours hanging up fancy, expensive outdoor Halloween lights, addressing and mailing their Halloween cards, and buying *haute-couture*-quality costumes for all their kids? Who cannot remember with a warm glow down-loading Jack-o-lantern patterns off the internet and then having the images of Freddy Kruger photo-engraved onto their pumpkins? Who cannot remember Mom buying bags of two-dollar candy bars for the neighbor-hood ghouls? Me neither.

The way I remember it, we carved a pumpkin the weekend before. A big toothy thing, obviously done by enthusiastic but unskilled children, not something that looks like Martha Stewart and her staff spent a week on it. Hanging spooky holiday decorations in the trees out-side our house never occurred to us. And when we went trick or treating, we were lucky to get a couple of candy bars the whole night. I think my mother gave out candy corn one year. One piece per child. I don't remember anyone complaining.

Not that my brothers and sisters were there to see her dole it out; we were all long gone trying to score as much swag as we could. The *good* houses, the ones that gave away especially unhealthy treats, we'd hit two or three times. I would visit first as a ghost with an old sheet over my head, then as a Roman senator in a sheet toga and for a third time as Lawrence of Arabia with the same sheet secured to my head Bedouin-style with a belt.

Most people think Halloween is the one day of the year when children can act like little devils and go around blackmailing adults into giving them treats but for my family, it was pretty much what we did every day, just without the costumes.

The scariest thing about Halloween today is what has happened to it. I don't want to sound like the Ghost of Halloween Past, but when did this fun, minor holiday get blown up into New Year's Eve, Christmas and Thanksgiving combined? If the greeting card companies and the retailers can do it to Halloween, they can do it to any holiday.

How long before we have to start buying our kids presents for the Summer Solstice? How are you decorating your house this year for Arbor Day? You say you don't have the time? Well, I don't *have* the time, either. I *make* the time.

How many people have you invited to your "People's Choice Award" night feast? Have you sent out your

Cinco de Mayo cards yet? What's the matter with you? It's only seven months away. Better get cracking.

And don't forget, if retailers have their way, you'll have to buy presents for every one of these holidays. Not just for your children, but for your spouse, for your siblings, for your in-laws, for your coworkers and your boss. Not just any old present, but something you will have to obsess over for weeks and weeks so as not to offend or appear unthoughtful.

If you give your sister the waffle iron for Groundhog Day instead of the neck massager she's been asking for, it could cause bad feelings for years. And isn't that the point of most holidays—to make you feel bad? Face it, if it's not stressing you, is it really a holiday?

If at First Class
You Don't Succeed . . .

A few years ago an airline lost a woman's cat in transit. They looked for that cat for twelve days before it finally turned up—alive and well and hungry. I'm glad that story had a happy ending but I couldn't shake the feeling that they had searched for the cat about eleven and a half days longer than they would have looked for a missing passenger. It seems the airlines do everything backwards. How many times have you had to sit on a long flight near one or more screaming babies? One baby can shred the nerves of several hundred passengers. Babies fly for free. Why? If allowed on the plane at all they should be charged triple.

When a flight gets cancelled, all the passengers on that flight are not put on the very next flight and the passengers on that flight pushed back, et cetera et cetera. Oh no, that would make too much sense. Instead the first set of passengers is pushed to the end of the line. What other business could get away with that?

On almost every flight I've taken the last few holidays some couple will show up at the very last minute and have to be ushered on board with special airline people hustling them through the door, stowing their hand luggage for them, getting them settled before rushing out so the crew could shut the cabin door. All under the hateful glare of the other passengers who had the courtesy to show up an hour early.

Guess whose luggage will come off first? The late passengers'. So why should they bother to show up on time when they get rewarded for their bad behavior? They didn't have to wait in any lines. They didn't have to hang around the lounge for an hour sitting in chairs that have been specifically designed to be uncomfortable so homeless people won't live in them. They didn't have to hear "Would Mr. and Mrs. Liptfitter please report to the main ticket counter?" forty times over the world's worst PA system. They didn't have to hear it because, of course, they are the Liptfitters.

"Honey, this is so nice, it's nice to be late," said Mr. Liptfitter.

"Late? What do you know about being late?" she snapped. "If you had listened to me we would have been two minutes later and they would have given us seats in First Class. Don't talk to me about being late. I know how to be late."

The shopkeepers in the airport hate the latecomers. They didn't have to spend four hours inside an airport with absolutely nothing to do but cruise the airport stores. Where else could you find a newsstand that sells such popular magazines as *Funeral Home Management*, *Cubicle Cloth Designer*, *Pension Fund Skimmer*, *Meter Reader Monthly*, and *Professional Llama Breeder*? What? No *Amateur Llama Breeder*? What kind of a dump are you running here?

The book stores are jammed with best-selling self-help books like *How to Pick a Self-Help Book*, *How To Get the Most Out of Self-Help Books*, *How to Get to the Front of this Store By Yourself,* and *Running a Billion Dollar Corporation Made Simple.*

You can also pick up a six-dollar container of three individually wrapped antacid tablets at any newsstand. Which you'll need because the only thing you can buy to eat in the entire airport without having to stand in an hour-long line is a frozen yogurt and a bag of cashews.

You'll never get into any of the good restaurants. Even if you do, you won't have time to eat there. Wait, isn't that the Liptfitters? They're sitting in the window of L'Exquisite, the fanciest restaurant in the entire airport. The line snakes from terminal A to terminal B and back again. How did they get in? They are laughing and drinking wine. She is eating medallions of beef with crab meat garnish. He is having the *coq au vin.*

I can't worry about it now. I have accidentally dragged my coat through something wet on the men's room floor while trying to juggle my carry-on luggage and use the sink at the same time. As I leave the men's room the Liptfitters glide past me on one of those beeping, chauffeur-driven electric carts that ferry elderly people around airports. Me, I rush back to my gate on foot. Just in time to see the Liptfitters disappear down the gangway with the rest of the First Class passengers.

Here's Looking at You, Kid

There's been a lot of back and forth about those full body scanners in airports that can see underneath your clothes. My wife is totally against it.

"I'm used to it," she said, "but for some poor fool just trying to do his job to have to see you naked for the first time . . . well, if they don't quit in disgust outright, it will probably spoil their appetite for days."

"Please. I have the body of an eighteen year-old."

"Yes, you do. A big, fat, out-of-shape, gray-haired eighteen year-old."

There's something about the black and white pictures from the airport scanners that is the opposite of sexy. Here's a thought experiment: imagine there was a rule that all airline passengers had to wear skin-tight Spandex to fly. Now think about your last trip to the airport and imagine everyone you saw in Spandex. Did you just taste a little vomit in your mouth?

If a *Sports Illustrated* swimsuit cover is a 10, the average body scan must be somewhere around a minus twenty. Face it, there is no amount of diet and exercise that is going to make Nana and Poppy flying back to Florida look sexy. Finally we have invented something that makes their driver's license photos look like glamour shots.

My cousin Maxine says she would never even think of submitting to a full body scan. "I'd be so embarrassed if some stranger saw me in my birthday suit." She told me this while we were on vacation in Virginia Beach. She was wearing two pieces of string and a large straw hat. The hat was fifty times bigger than her bathing suit. I've seen pole dancers that wear more clothes. We were sunning on the deck as all manner of people walked by on their way to the beach, all of them complete strangers.

When I was young, people used to dress up to fly. You'd wear your best clothes to the airport, you'd put on sophisticated airs and act as if you'd been on a plane many times before, even if this was your first flight. There was a time when seatbelts were a novelty and yes, you did have to pay attention to find out how they worked. The stewardess (flight attendants were way in the future) would ask you if you had flown before.

"All the time," I would say as my hands shook. Stewardesses were famous for being young and glamorous. For years it was considered one of the best jobs a woman could have. The apartments where they lived when they weren't off to Swingin' London or Paris and Rome were called "stew zoos" and every single man in town knew to hang out in nearby bars. You wanted to make a good impression when you flew.

Now when I take a flight I expect to see a sign at the check-in counter that says "No Shirt, No Shoes, No Problem."

Now people dress like they are going to the gym to get on a plane. Sweat pants, check. Sleeveless t-shirt, check. Sockless trainers, check. Is going through the body scanner any more revealing than the clothes people wear to the gym and the beach every day?

Still, a full body scan is way past many people's comfort level. But there may be an easy solution. Make the TSA employees at the gate wear Speedos and bikinis, because what is good for the goose is good for the scanner.

This Way to Baggage Ransom

I'm not against airlines charging extra for bags. I've seen passengers show up at the airport with seven bags for a weekend trip. Lewis and Clark didn't pack this much luggage. These people aren't traveling, they're moving. Recently I saw a soldier getting ready to travel to Iraq for a six-month tour of duty with just a duffle bag; standing behind him in line were two parents and a small child on their way to Orlando for a few days. It took two porters to get all their luggage to the check-in. And that's not counting the carry-on toy bag, the sippy cups, the snack bag, and the child seat.

Here's a little travel rule of thumb: if you have so much luggage that you can fill up a U-Haul—then rent one. If you really need all that stuff, and if you're going to be away from your home for three or four months, why fly? It's not as if you're in a rush. Do everyone a favor and take your car.

Even though the airlines have a point about luggage, once the airlines feel comfortable charging for "extra" luggage, they will find other ways to nickel and twenty-five dollar us to death. How long before some airline floats the idea of a "gangway charge" for walking between the terminal and the plane? Want to sit in the waiting room? Ten bucks. Passengers needing assistance can board first—right after they fork over a twenty-five dollar wheelchair rental charge. Charge your laptop? Sure, just show us your fifteen-dollar electrical outlet usage permit.

"Have you heard about our exciting new 'waiting on the tarmac' plan? The longer you wait, the less you pay. Ten dollars for the first hour, nine for the second and so on. The tenth hour is absolutely FREE! Terms and conditions listed below. This offer may not be legal in your state."

"Would you like to know if your flight has been delayed or cancelled? Five dollars, please."

"Sir, we've just charged you fifty dollars for your over-weight luggage, now if you wouldn't mind standing on our scale . . ."

I'm afraid to say any more; some airline executive may be reading this and I don't want to give them any ideas they don't already have.

Actually, there is one thing they should charge extra for. If it makes sense to charge passengers twenty-five dollars for extra luggage—luggage that is going to sit quietly in the luggage compartment not causing any problems, luggage that is not expecting to get a bag of pretzels or a soft drink or wanting to see an in-flight movie—then charge for screaming, crying babies that now fly for free.

Most airlines don't charge for infants too small to sit anywhere but their mother's lap, the theory being they are only using one seat. But infants don't use just one seat. At the minimum, a passenger who travels with an infant should pay for the six seats nearest to them. If the baby's parents can sell the seats to friends and relatives who don't mind the diaper changing and the crying, fine, but no way should infants be allowed to fly for free.

And even after they start charging extra for infants, the airlines should limit how many babies there can be on any one flight. Kind of like First Class in reverse.

"Whoops! I'm sorry, our Screaming Baby section is full on this flight, we'll see if we can get you on the next flight. Of course, we'll have to charge you a twenty-five dollar rebooking fee."

Club Tarmac

Big, big decisions. Sue and I don't get that much time off, so we spend a lot of time planning which tarmac we want to spend our vacation on each year.

I like O'Hare, but Sue prefers Atlanta for some reason. Maybe we could compromise. Who doesn't love Newark? It's easy to get to, and it has that nifty monorail that you can watch from your seat in the plane.

"What about Dulles? Remember that time we spent nine hours out there that Memorial Day Weekend? It was only ninety-two outside, but inside it was one hundred and twenty. It was like being in the Sahara without all the bother of going there. The people behind us were seeing an imaginary oasis. Too bad our pictures didn't come out. Our digital camera melted. That one of the flight attendants holding down that guy who was missing his mother's funeral was pretty dramatic. And entertaining. Better than anything we'd have seen in Canada, which is where we were actually supposed to be. They gave us two free tickets to the LAX tarmac, which reminds me, we should use those before our airline goes belly up, which with all the lawsuits might be any day now."

"I know," says Sue, "But sitting on the tarmac in California scares me. What if there's an earthquake? It could shake the overflowing toilets into the cabin and spoil everyone's fun."

"What about Paris? Or Barcelona? I hear great things about their airports."

"There's a problem. I don't think they let their planes sit on the tarmac for nine or ten hours in other, more backward countries. Once you leave the U.S., you're pretty much at the mercy of those radical, overseas governments. I don't even think they allow overbooking."

"The Socialists."

"You know the great thing about tarmac vacations? You don't have to pack any luggage, you don't have to rent a car, you don't have to reserve a hotel room. It's all right there for us in one little package. About the only expense is bribing the flight attendants for food and water."

"Yeah, I kept expecting to see Jeff Probst from *Survivor* come down the aisles and separate us into tribes. That's part of the fun, when people start to go stir crazy."

"If only we could buy some coach airline seats for our living room."

"Who would ever bother to fly if you could sit in those things at home?"

"Of course, not every tarmac vacation is fun. Remember that time we got the chatty pilot? 'Ladies and Gentlemen, there's been a weather delay in Albany, we should be off the ground in about twenty minutes.' What's up with that? Who wants to know all that stuff? I swear, that guy would not stop talking. I'll bet you he made a so-called 'important' announcement at least once an hour."

"Thank goodness most pilots don't bother you with all that stuff. Nine, ten hours without a word about why we're sitting here, that's the way it should be."

"What I like is that parents get to spend some quality time with their kids. Especially the babies. If you can't bond with your children after nine hours locked in a 747, well, you're just not trying."

"And it's a great way to meet people. Like what's-her-name who was sitting in the window seat next to us on the tarmac at Dallas-Ft. Worth. It's too bad she missed her connecting flight to her fantasy vacation in Greece that she's been saving and planning for years, but that's the thing about Club Tarmac. It's always a surprise."

"Some people just can't deal with spontaneity. I get enough rules and regulations at work. When I'm on vacation I like to go with the flow, let other people make all the decisions for a change."

"Yes, I don't get all the complaining. What is it about 'Buy one tarmac vacation and get one free,' that people don't understand? I mean, get real. If it was really important for you to be somewhere, exactly at a certain time on a certain day, why on Earth would you ever use an airline?"

The First Thanksgiving Family Feud

Historians all agree—the Pilgrim's First Thanksgiving was a one-time event. It wasn't turned into a yearly celebration until Abraham Lincoln made it official during the middle of the Civil War, almost 250 years later. A newly-discovered cache of papers composed by the original passengers of the Mayflower may explain why.

"Never again," writes John Alden. "Six long hours we have spent looking at the hind end of a horse on the overly crowded road to the house of my parents and lo, for what? To see my brother with whom I barely speak and his harpy wyfe who so disrespecteth me and mine in a backhanded way? He starteth acting like a wee childe from the time we stepped from the carriage until the time we departed. He bringeth up small jealousies and grievances from our youth long ago. His unhappiness is like a contagion, a pustule that never heals. 'Letteth it go and getteth a life,' he has made me wish to scream, and more times than one.

"One unpleasantry follows another as I suffer my uncles and aunts to runneth on and on about my cousins— how well they are doing, how much money they are sending to their parents, what comely grandchildren they have produced. Yet I knoweth these same cousins. They would soil themselves if they were ever made to do a day's work.

"They wish their parents dead and spend their days making plans to squander their inheritance in a warmer clime. Their small children hear not the word 'no' and understandeth not its meaning. They runneth around and screameth all day when peace and quiet is called for.

"And my wyfe cares not for the way my mother prepareth the meal. 'She useth not oysters in the fowl's stuffing,' she rails at me. 'She putteth not the bird in a paper bag in the hearth.' It maketh me fatigued to hear such words. Yet Priscilla's own stuffing would not winneth any prize, even in the land of my birth where they can taste not the difference between soup and soap. She knoweth not, but secretly I giveth my portions of her bounty to the hound beneath the table. It teacheth him not to beg.

"My wyfe speaks ill of none, yet I can tell from the bearing of her body that she would rather be ducking witches on a cold day in December than be in the company of my family and their offspring. As if her family be a barrel of salted fish. Her sisters make it well known that their spouses buy them more kitchen tools than I, and that the corn from their labor is bigger and better than that of my own. They maketh my head hurt. Were they not aboard, the journey of the Mayflower could have been as a fun ship. With them, it was as the hate boat.

"It occurred to me suddenly that we may have left the wood stove on at home. Priscilla volunteered that it may be true as she had often noticed my forgetful habits. Happily, we fled the festivities. On the road home we sat in silence for many hours. 'Let us hope we can do this again next year,' at last I spoke. It got a hearty laugh as

Priscilla knew I was in perfect jest. In truth, you could not make us do that again were two hundred and fifty years to pass. And for that we gave thanks."

Sex and the
Single High Schooler

This year my cousin Joe and I were at the same holiday table together for the first time in five years. We reminisced about sitting together at the kids' table with all our brothers and sisters long ago. Catching up with each other, Joe proudly pulled out a picture of his daughter from his wallet. It was T'fanny's high school yearbook photo. Joe lives out of state; I haven't seen the child since she was ten or eleven. In the photo T'fanny is lying on her side, her head resting on one arm which is languidly stretched out above her. It looks as if she were auditioning for Ann-Margaret's part in a remake of "Kitten with a Whip." Her lips are pursed, her eyes are dreamy, her index finger is curled in a "come here, big boy" motion.

T'fanny is wearing a spaghetti strap top and she is showing more cleavage than a three-hundred-pound plumber working in a tight crawl space. Lon Chaney wore less make-up in *The Hunchback of Notre Dame*.

I wondered what her classmates' photos must look like. What if T'fanny is the shy, tame one? What do the out-of-control girls in her class look like? What did the jocks wear for their pictures? Jocks? Do they sell this yearbook under the counter? Does it come in a plain brown wrapper? Does it have a centerfold? If they find me with one will I be charged with possessing child pornography? What messages could her friends possibly write under a picture like that? "Hope your dream will come true and you'll get to be a tramp in a biker bar!"

"What classes did she take?" I asked Joe. "Pole Dancing 101? How to Run an Escort Service? Holding Cell Etiquette? Don't you find this inappropriate and offensive?"

"Times have changed since we were kids," Joe explained as if I were some pathetic, out-of-touch old man who still squirts children with a garden hose when they walk past his house. "Life is tougher now, kids are under a lot of pressure."

"Who is pressuring them? Their pimps? What has pressure got to do with dressing like a hooker? And so what if I squirt a few children with a garden hose. It teaches them to stay off my lawn."

"Things have changed since you sat for your high school daguerreotype. You don't have to stand still anymore without blinking for two minutes. They don't use glass plates anymore. Kids know how to work the camera today."

Joe's right, our senior photographs were embarrassing. It's hard to believe we actually had to pay someone to make us look that bad. Instead of asking who was the best photographer in town, our school principal asked who was the cheapest. The only way the photographer could have made us look more dated was if he had made us wear raccoon coats and wave triangular school pennants.

The good news is that we were not alone. Every school across the country seems to have hired the same photographer. There is an ad on the internet using yearbook photos to get people to look up out-of-touch classmates. Every time I see it, I swear they are using pictures out of my very own yearbook. The haircuts, the clothes, the glasses all look the same. And yet the pictures come from another school, halfway across the country.

I wonder if someday T'fanny will be as embarrassed by her yearbook photograph as I am of mine. One day, will one of T'fanny's children find her yearbook in the bottom of a closet and say, "Hey, Stepmom, is that really you? You mean you had to wear clothes to school back then? I'm so glad we go to All Nude High. We're not distracted by who's wearing what the way you guys were. We don't have any of that bickering about who has better clothes than who. It's just a much friendlier, relaxed way to learn. And we don't pay them to take our graduation pictures. They pay us."

Death of the Party

Aunt Ethel has a rule that whenever we have a get-together at her house we can only talk about our diseases and medications for the first fifteen minutes. After that we have to change the subject.

Fifteen minutes is hardly enough time to describe the procedure to replace my pacemaker, much less go into my sciatica—especially if everyone else is going to keep butting in with tales of their bypasses and blood clots and deep vein thromboses and knee replacements and shingles and carpal tunnel surgeries.

But because of Ethel's rules, we have all edited down our tales to two minutes per couple. Much to Sue's embarrassment, I find showing my scars an easy way to speed up the telling of my story, a visual aid, so to speak. I am a walking Power Point presentation.

My scars are testament to my suffering even though I didn't suffer very much. I got them all while I was under plenty of anesthesia and on the best pain relievers health insurance can buy, but I don't much see the point in including that in my allotted time. I prefer my version where they poured whiskey down my throat and made me bite down on a stick of wood while they eviscerated me.

Being unhealthy is a competition for men. A guy who has a quadruple bypass is much more macho than a guy who has only had a triple. The man who only needs to lose twenty pounds is a wimp compared to the guy whose doctor told him he had to lose a hundred and twenty or he would surely die on his way home from the office.

An operation that lasts eighteen hours and needed twelve surgeons is much better than one that only lasted three hours. In short, the unhealthier you are, the less you take care of yourself, the better your medical stories.

You'd think the guys with the worst, most debilitating, most painful, most expensive diseases would be hooked up to all kinds of beeping monitors, strapped to a hospital bed in intensive care. They are not. They are out golfing with me. I think their diseases are actually making them live longer because they clearly live to talk about them.

John, who consistently out-drives me, who consistently beats me, can barely get out of the golf cart. He has bad knees, a bad back, a bad heart, diabetes, high blood pressure, sleep apnea, arthritis, and tennis elbow. I know this because that's all he talks about.

My other partners are as bad or worse. They will never die. Unless they had to go to one of Ethel's parties where they couldn't talk about everything that ails them. *That* would kill them. Younger golfers in much better shape have long passed away while these guys live on and on and on. I should make it a rule on the golf course that you can only talk about your medical condition for one hole.

I pity the middle-aged man who is in good health because he has no stories to tell; he has no allergies, he doesn't know his blood sugar level, he can do deep knee bends with no problem, he has no lower back pain, he doesn't take any prescription meds, he's heard of Lipitor but doesn't quite know why you would take it.

That is a man you do not want to sit next to at dinner. He has zero entertainment value. He's missing out on a huge part of the fun of getting old. I long for the day when I can hear how much his prescriptions cost and how much he really pays.

"Three hundred and eighty dollars for thirty pills. And you know what I paid? Guess? Go ahead, guess. Two dollars and seventy-five cents!" If you can't top that, just shut up and eat. If you have had a recent heart-lung transplant, however, now would be a good time to bring it up. And how much it cost. Down to the penny. That's entertainment. But keep it to fifteen minutes.

The Kids' Table

"Ashley will eat meat, but not if it looks like the animal that it comes from."

My sister-in-law was explaining why her daughter would eat fish sticks, but not fish. She would eat chicken nuggets but not chicken wings. Ashley would eat hamburger but not beef tongue. Actually, as soon as we said "beef tongue" the poor child turned green.

"That is disgusting," she said.

"So that would be a 'no' on pig's feet, but a 'yes' on ham salad?" I asked. Ashley, a high school senior, gave me the "why do I even bother to speak to people who aren't my exact same age" look, pushed back her chair and made her way toward the dessert table.

We were at a gigantic family holiday get-together, with a long buffet of dishes brought to pass: turkey, ham,

47

salads, and pies. Ashley's cousin, Ashleigh, who is almost the same age as Ashley and wears her hair exactly the same way and gets very upset when people who haven't seen her in five years confuse her with Ashley, was also sitting at our table. I asked her mother if there was anything Ashleigh wouldn't eat.

"Basically, no mixing of food. She'll eat spaghetti without sauce. Bones. She won't eat anything with a bone in it. No steak, no ham. Fish. She won't eat fish at all."

"Mussels? Squid?" I asked.

"No way," exclaimed Ashleigh. Fine, more calamari for the rest of us. Her plate was filled with potato salad, mashed potatoes and scalloped potatoes. The green bits of pepper from the potato salad had been carefully scouted out and pushed to one little spot on her plate.

Table-hopping, I ran into Ashley and Ashleigh's cousin Ashlee. Ashlee was busy mashing her lasagna into mush. It looked like baby food lasagna after she was finished with it. But Ashlee was only twelve, a mere child; that explains why she was still eating baby food. It did not explain why a thong was peeking out over the back of her low cut jeans.

Ashlee is what advertisers call a "tween." Tweens are pre-teenagers, in between children and teenagers. Not quite a teenager, but just as annoying. According to big advertising agencies, tweens set the family budget; they are the most desirable demographic in the world.

It seems Ashlee and her little friends are the engine that drives our economy. We old people have negative advertising value. It's pretty ego-deflating to suddenly learn that even though we have enough money to buy a house, a car, and vacation every now and then, advertisers don't want us anymore. They've jilted us for our sleep-until-noon, eye-rolling, self-absorbed children. And why did the advertising gurus ditch their pathetic, old, workaholic, allowance-giving friends? Because there's a tween born every minute. You can sell them anything. Except food that looks like the animal it came from.

My two other nieces, ten-year-old Ashlie and eleven-year-old Ashlea, stopped by to say hello. Not to me, but to whomever they were talking to on their state-of-the-art smart phones. Last year, between us, Sue and I didn't use our cell phones as much as these two kids did during dinner. Sue and I wondered what calling plan the tweens were on. It had to be better than ours. So were their phones. Mine was three years old already. It was huge and clunky, almost ten ounces and half the size of a pack of cigarettes. Ashlea and Ashlie both had brand new iPhones that they'd bought with their allowance debit cards.

"Why on Earth would you want a phone that could take pictures?" I asked Sue. At that moment, Ashlea bent over and took a picture of my plate, which was piled high with all that good, calorie-laden stuff I can't get at home. It was full of bones and wings and food touching other food, dripping with gravies and sauces.

"I'm sending this to our cousins Haley, Hailey, Haylee, Haleigh, Hailee, Halie, and Hali. They won't believe what some people will put in their mouths."

Thinking Outside the Gift-wrapped Box

For once, I have finished my Christmas shopping early. I just went over my list to make sure that I hadn't forgotten anyone. It was pretty easy; this year, everybody's getting the same thing from me. Nothing.

It really saves on the wrapping paper and the trips to the store. And it lets me avoid Black Friday altogether. By giving my friends and family the gift of nothing, they won't have to wrap anything for me; they can sit home on Black Friday and putter around the house, relax, spend time with their spouses and children. They won't have to wait in line at the Post Office; they won't have to risk being trampled in shopping-frenzy crowds; they won't have to circle the mall parking lot for twenty minutes trying to find a spot. In short, the gift of nothing is not a chintzy gift. It will save my friends and family time and money because they will also be giving me the gift of nothing. I was never any good at tying bows, anyway. I expect I will get long, effusive thank you notes from people for having the guts to give them the gift of nothing.

Sue is not so sure. She thinks I will be shunned. It's a chance I'm willing to take. Will Aunt Ethel be upset because I didn't get her a chocolate fondue maker?

Others have told me I'm wrecking the economy. If you believe the TV news, you'd think that if we don't buy a ton of worthless junk on Black Friday we are letting our country down, that we are unpatriotic for not buying a scarf for Aunt Minnie and a tie for Uncle Bob. "Will more people shop this year than last year?" they ask. "Will they spend more than last year?" It seems they are confusing Christmas with a football game, that somehow the country that buys the most presents wins. Wins what? More credit card debt? More time in the car? More stress? Exactly what do we win? Your life is not crazy enough, you want to add to it? And you're not helping our economy— the scarf and the tie were made in Bangladesh. You're helping their economy and they don't even celebrate Christmas.

The gift of nothing may sound like a dodge to get out of buying gifts for my friends, my family, and my co-workers, and I admit, I do not like shopping. But the gift of nothing only works if you tell people that's what you are giving them. Some people will understand right away that this is a substantial gift, that you are one less person they have to shop for, one less thing they have to think about. If you can't bring yourself to buy nothing, spend Black Friday baking cookies. Homemade cookies, there's something you can't buy in a store; there's something that didn't come from overseas.

With children living at home, it's different; they won't understand the gift of nothing, but they will understand that Santa's sleigh can only carry so many things, and if you ask for ten things, that means that other children can only get one thing. Or nothing.

Thanksgiving is the perfect time to mention that you're planning to give the gift of nothing this year. You'll be surprised at how many of your nearest and dearest will say, "Thank you, for years I've wanted to take Christmas back and make it a family gathering, not a competition about who can spend the most. I can't stand what it's turned into."

Make this year the year you don't have to worry about buying something that is the wrong size or the wrong color or something that they already have or something they will have to return. Make this the year to swear off buying trinkets just for the sake of buying. If you think giving someone a gift says "I love you," guess what? So does saying, "I love you." I can only remember a few gifts I've been given over the years, but I can remember every time someone hugged me and said "I love you." It's a huge gift that costs nothing and for all your money, you can't buy it at Neiman-Marcus.

Merry Christmas, Inc.

The Christmas card from our bank is on the mantel with all the other Christmas cards: the ones from the credit card companies, the one from the auto dealer, the one from the mortgage company, the ones from the charities we stopped giving money to fifteen years ago, the one from our senator, the one from our congressman, the one from a hotel chain we stayed at once, the one from Recliner City, and the one from our cell phone provider. Yet they say no one has the Christmas spirit any more.

I thought my mortgage company was your typical cold, hard-hearted, bottom-line conglomerate, and then we received this bright red and gold Christmas card that says "From your friends at First Financial." How I misjudged them. It turns out I have many dear, close friends there. Why, there's what's-her-face and what's-his-name—that guy with the toupee—Bob or Charlie or Pete or something. I don't know why we've never had them over for dinner. Maybe it's because we've had no contact with them whatsoever in the six years since the closing. Who could miss the personalized seasonal message they put on the bulk rate meter stamp: "Can You Save Money by Refinancing this Season?"

Our auto dealer's card had a picture of all their salesmen wearing Santa hats gathered around their latest, shiny, fire-engine-red sports car. "'Tis the Season to drop in and test drive the brand-new Labrador. It's big and friendly and loves attention! Buy one today! From Santa's Helpers at the New and Used Auto Warehouse!" It was addressed to "Resident." It made me feel all warm and fuzzy inside to know they're full of the Christmas spirit. I guess we have to send them a card now. We got one from the Tire Barn, too. Better add them to the list.

Our stockbroker sent us two cards, one for my 401k and one for my regular account. That's so thoughtful. How does he remember? He must have a brain like a computer. And such an expensive-looking card. Five dollars apiece, I would think. I wonder where he gets all the money? The broker's card covers all the holiday bases; it says "Happy Holidays," "Merry Christmas," "Happy Hanukkah," "Feliz Navidad," "Joyeux Noel," "Kwanzaa Yenu Iwe Na Heri," and "Gajan Kristnaskon." His pagan customers must be miffed that there's no "Have a Festive Saturnalia," but you can't please everyone.

I do a lot of business online, so I get a lot of online Christmas cards from people who have my credit card number and my e-mail address. It's becoming a long list. Should I print out their cards or just leave them on the computer? Some of them sing and dance. Don't you love it when you're supposed to be hard at work and you open an e-mail and then, at double the volume of anything else going on in the office a bunch of barking dogs start singing "Jingle Bells"? My boss had the bonus envelopes in his hand when that happened. Now I'll never know what mine would have been.

I do get a lot of cards from old friends and far-flung family members, but they rarely contain any coupons or an offer for a free, three-day visit to a time-share like the cards my corporate friends send me, or ten percent off last Christmas's hot toy. I want to call up my cheap relatives and say, "Hey, what's the matter with you? Don't you know the true meaning of Christmas? I'm taking you off my Christmas card list," but then I calm down and ask myself, "What would my big box store do?" They never take *anyone* off their Christmas card list.

A Newsletter Too Far:

Well, it's that time of year again. The Fergusons have had a great year. As you can see, Bob lost forty pounds on the Atkins diet. He had to get a second job to stay on it because he eats more red meat than a grizzly bear but you can't knock the results. We've spent so much on food this year we can't afford to buy him new clothes. His pants are so baggy he looks like he just graduated from clown school. Still, it beats the stomach staple the doctors were talking about and he says he feels good.

Speaking of health, Amber's nose ring got infected and she missed most of this last semester at junior college. The whole experience has made her think seriously of changing her major from Tattoo Art Appreciation to Herbal Holistic Aromatherapist, but nothing's firm yet.

The real exciting news is that Amber has a boyfriend, a lawyer. No, wait a minute. Bob says the boyfriend isn't a lawyer, the boyfriend *has* a lawyer. My bad. Kids these days, I could never have afforded a lawyer when I was his age. He must really be smart. He's living out above our garage until the heat dies down. We used to have an apartment like that, too. Once the heat came on you could never turn it off.

Bob's mother is still living. With us. Sometimes she's a little forgetful. I can't tell you how often I have to remind her that she's living in my house. I think she would probably be better off in a nursing home but Bob won't hear of it. He's just that kind of guy. He says, "As long as you're healthy, why shouldn't she stay with us?" Except for the smoking, the drinking, the cleaning, and the laundry she's not much of a bother.

I suppose this is as good a time as any to explain that newspaper headline in June, "Bob Ferguson Arrested in Credit Card Fraud." Actually it was good news; they arrested the guy who had stolen Bob's identity. They caught him trying to charge a Slim Jim and a box of Handi-Wipes down at the Gas and Go Away. Little did the thief know that Bob's credit cards have been maxed out for months and all the clerks have orders to call the police if he ever tries to use a credit card there again.

The guy pretending to be Bob is still in jail, but that will probably change when they find out about the back taxes we owe on that phony tax shelter scam we got involved in last year. It seems that just because you don't mow your back yard doesn't mean you can call it a "Tree Farm" and start taking an agricultural deduction. Who knew? If the fake Bob Ferguson wants to do eight to ten years for tax fraud, that's fine with us.

Well, that's about it from the Fergusons. I've got to go pick up Fluffy from the vet. I'm not sure I want to see the bill. Well, how much could a simple tail reattachment cost, anyway?

Wishing you and yours a Happy Holiday,

The Fergusons

Why You Should Screen Your Holiday Calls

"Hey, it's me. I keep getting your message machine. Did you get the one I left yesterday? I know it's short notice, but I'll be arriving tomorrow on the three o'clock flight. You can just pick me up at the baggage claim, no need to park, I like to make things easy. I don't want anyone fussing over me while I'm there. Just tell me where the fridge is, where the espresso maker is, where the whirlpool spa is, where the liquor cabinet is, where the wine cellar is, where your flat screen plasma HDTV is and I'm pretty much good to go. You may not even know I'm there. Don't let me interfere in any way.

I usually take breakfast at 9:30 or so and read the paper. Nothing fancy, Eggs Benedict, *Pain Perdu* or Belgian waffles with fresh fruit will do just fine. Or maybe an egg white omelet with sautéed wild mushrooms and shallots, but don't go baking fresh bread every morning unless that's what you normally do. Treat me like I'm one of the family. In a way, I am. I nearly married your second cousin twenty years ago and if that doesn't make me family, what does?

I was planning to visit Trish and Chuck this year like I did two years ago, but they had to take a sudden last-minute trip to Bosnia. It's funny, almost everyone I know was traveling or having elective surgery the only three weeks I have free. But that's OK, I retire next year and I'll be able to travel any time I want. I'll be able to fit into anyone's schedule. Won't that be great?

You do have hypoallergenic pillows, don't you? That's all right, there's plenty of time to run out and get some. Did I tell you about that week I spent with Aunt Edna? Absolutely dreadful. I didn't even have my own bathroom. I had to share it with a complete stranger. Her son or daughter or somebody. I didn't say anything, but really, what has happened to common courtesy in this country?

Actually, I think Edna was suffering from what they call "Holiday Depression." A lot of people get that this time of year. No one's really sure what causes it, but let me tell you, I see a lot of it. I was telling Edna about my sciatica and suddenly she stood up and yelled, "Make it stop! I can't take it anymore!" The poor, sick, deluded woman. I wanted to stay and nurse her back to health, but Uncle Paul insisted all she needed was a good rest and we'd have to cut my visit short.

I said I wouldn't think of it, that I would stay and help nurse Aunt Edna back to health. But he offered to put me up in a four-star hotel downtown and what could I say? She really does need to get some professional help. Besides, they're not really family, not the way we are.

See you tomorrow. Bye!

The Perfectarian

tarting a few weeks before the holiday, you'll see a
spate of TV shows, columns and magazine stories
that will tell you how to make the "perfect" turkey. They'll explain how to roast it in a paper bag, how
to bake it upside down, how to deep-fat fry it, how to
put it on a rotisserie, smother it in mustard, blacken it,
debone it and cook just the pieces, stuff it with bread,
rice, oysters, onions, mushrooms, squash, or a duck and
a chicken. Or stuff it not at all. I have no quibble with
that; I have enjoyed turkey almost every way possible
there is to prepare one. The thing that bothers me is that
they all want you to be "perfect."

Have you ever been to a Thanksgiving dinner where a
guest pushed back his chair, stood up, slapped his napkin
down on the table in a fit of righteous disgust and

snarled to the hostess, "I'm leaving, don't ever invite me here again, that turkey is not perfect!"

Nothing else about the holiday will be perfect; why should the turkey be any different? Was waiting in the airport lounge for ten hours perfect? Was the traffic jam on the way to grandma's house perfect? Did the kids behave perfectly? Is everything you eat perfect? Was that egg you had for breakfast yesterday at the Dirty Fork Diner perfect? What? You ate it anyway? Was that left-over lasagna you had for dinner last night perfect or were the edges a little crispy, the cheese a little dry? Did you just hold your nose and eat it anyway? Did you force yourself to have two pieces the way I did? Are the TV shows that tell you how to make the perfect turkey perfect?

The implication is that if your turkey is not perfect you have failed your friends and family, you will have spoiled everyone's holiday, you have stolen all the joy from the world, you have wrecked everyone's life, now and forever. Yet I can say from years of experience that cooking the perfect turkey and cooking any old turkey any old way has about the same effect on the festivities. That's the great thing about turkey—it's hard to mess up. Unless you forget to thaw it, which I think I have done more than once. Even then, the same people keep coming back, year after year.

Unless you've done something really ghastly to it, say, experimental turkey sashimi or turkey on a stick or turkey tartar or tofurkey or turkey in lime Jell-O or turkey ice cream, people will still eat it and even if they don't, they will talk about it for years, and they will still come back year after year to see what crazy thing you'll do next.

When did perfection become the standard for the holidays instead of happiness and fun? Perfection is highly overrated. My Dad used to get up on a rickety ladder and spend a few hours each year putting up a simple string of colored lights on our front porch every Christmas. The bulbs were bulky and ugly compared to the kind you can buy today and if one light on the string went out, they all went out. It was a tedious all-day affair trying to find out which bulb had burned out. After my sixth or seventh sibling showed up, Dad didn't even bother with the outside of the house. Yet in all those years, no one ever knocked on our front door and said, "What's with the pathetic light show? You guys aren't even trying. The guy down the street, his are perfect." All the perfect guy's kids were at our house, making a mess, enjoying not being perfect.

Our tree was the opposite of the perfect trees you will see in the magazines. We kids hung the decorations and the tinsel so that up to the halfway point, the tree was over-decorated and above that it was under-decorated. It did not look like any of the trees you saw in the magazines, yet I don't remember anyone remarking "Why, that's the ugliest thing I've ever seen. It looks like you let a bunch of children decorate it!" It never occurred to us that it wasn't perfect.

My mother was big on watering the tree every day. I remember asking her why. "That way," she explained, "it will live longer." For years I thought that adding water to things would keep them alive. Dead dog, add water. Dead fish, add water. It was a long time before I realized it was cutting down the tree that killed it, not a lack of water.

My grandfather always gave me a brand new wallet each Christmas. I don't know what he thought I needed one for when I was six. My driver's license? Not the perfect gift, but I remember it still.

When they found my grandfather, they never could figure out why the carpet around his body was so wet.

Mom tried a new recipe one year for fruitcake. She knew no one really liked fruitcake, so she found this recipe that was all dried fruit and nuts and no cake. I don't remember what held it all together, I think she just threw candied fruit and nuts into a bubbling pot of corn syrup and cooked it until it fused together like molten glass. To get a piece small enough to eat, you had to shatter it with a hammer. It never stopped us from eating it. It was far from perfect, but no one complained.

The next time you see an anorexic morning show co-host who is working his or her way through their third marriage and has two teenagers in rehab and who just sat through an hour of hair and make-up say, "And coming up next, how to make the perfect holiday turkey," you should ask yourself, "How has all that perfection worked out for them?" If making the perfect turkey still has you tied up in knots, here's a foolproof, can't-go-wrong, sure-fire, crowd-pleasing dinner suggestion. Serve ham.

At Play in the Fields
of O'Hare

There are two ways to travel: First Class or with
children. —*Robert Benchley*

"The flat escalators at the airport are my favorite
thing to play on. My sister Chrissy and me
like to run in the wrong direction on them
while big people try to get around us. It's like a Disney
ride but you don't have to wait in line. But a lot of times
grown-ups don't even know it's a ride. Sometimes they
don't even get on the escalators and walk in the boring
old aisles even though they can see us having lots of fun
on them. Other times they say things like 'This is not a
playground, you could get hurt. Where are your parents?'

"Clean your glasses, mister. They're standing right over there. Dad's reading the newspaper. Mom's on the her cell phone. Hey, you want to run up the down escalator with me? Never mind, watch this. I can hang on this black, rubbery moving thing and then let it drag me along this flat escalator. No, you can't do it, Chrissy. I just invented it and it's mine. Mom. Mom! MOM! MMMOMMM! Chrissy won't stop it!

"I got brand new wheelie shoes. They're like sneakers and roller skates all in one. Watch this. Watch, mom, watch! Mom. Mom! MOM! MMMOMMM!

"Too late. They never seem to be watching when I do the coolest stuff, like skate in and out of that line of people over there. It's like I'm invisible. Want to see me ram this shopping cart thingy into a window real hard? Watch!

"Wow! Did you see that! The whole window shook. Did you see that old lady jump? Did you see everybody watching me? Except Mom and Dad. They miss all the good stuff. Mom! Mom! Mom, watch me! MOM! MMMOMMMM! Look!

"This is soooo boring. Mom. Mom! MOM! Get me another soda. I put this one down on the seat and it fell over. And I had only taken one sip. Now it's gone. Let's sit somewhere else. This is all messy!

"I don't WANT to play with Chrissy! NO, NO, NO, NO, NO, NO! THIS *IS* MY INDOOR VOICE! MMMOMMM!

"I don't have to go to the bathroom. I'm fine. I'm telling you, it's OK. I'm positive.

"Chrissy, watch this. When I push this door open, it starts all those bells ringing. You try it. See? What'd I tell you? Have you ever heard anything that loud? Why is everybody running? Mom. Mom. Mom! MOM! MMMOMMM!

"I don't care that we have to get on the plane right now. *I* have to go to the bathroom RIGHT NOW! Do you know what I mean?

"Look at this, I can make all the sinks turn on at once. See that? Dad? Dad! DAD! DDDADDD!

"What do you mean they wouldn't hold the plane for us? They just left? Can't we sue them, Dad? Can't we?

Can't we? Like we sued that old school bus driver? You mean you settled for an upgrade to First Class on the next flight? OK. Just like last time, huh, Dad. Dad! DAD! DDDADDD!"

Home for the Holidays, We Think

Jackson has been home on his holiday break from college for two weeks now. His parents are over the moon about it—you'd almost think they had seen him.

"We know he's here," beamed Millie. "There are dirty clothes are all over his bathroom and the kitchen looks like we had one of those bear attacks you see on the news. Certainly a stranger wouldn't sneak into our house and throw ugly, smelly clothes on our floor, would they? It has to be Jack. It's so good to have him back home."

There is mounting evidence that he is actually at home, or at least in town. Giant, muddy footprints trail across the living room carpet. There are turkey bones

and half-eaten bags of chips and crackers strewn around
the house, treasured possessions are randomly broken,
missing or moved, seemingly without rhyme or reason.
One car is missing, the other has its fender hanging by a
bolt.

"Maybe you should report the car stolen," I said. "And
have security cameras installed in your kitchen. Channel
Eleven would pay a lot for real video of a bear trashing
your kitchen."

"It wasn't a bear," said Dan, Jack's father. "Bears don't
know how to use pop tops. Besides, we know he's
around—a lot of the girls he went to high school with
that we haven't heard from in months are suddenly calling, leaving messages. What does 'IM me' mean? Of
course I'm me."

"His bed looks slept in—by several people," Millie
added. Then suddenly a shadow passed over her face. "I
hope he's not having group sex. Yet. He's so immature
about some things. I don't want him to be hurt."

"Yeah, I hear it's painful." I said. "I still don't understand why you're so sure it's Jack eating your food, steal-
ing your car, and destroying your house. Remember that

scene at the Swanson's last Christmas? Ed came down for breakfast and saw his son Chuck sleeping on the sofa, then Betty comes down for breakfast and sees Chuck sleeping on the sofa.

"Rough night," she says to Ed. They laugh, remembering their own college years, when the phone rings. It's Chuck telling them he's sorry he missed his flight, he'll be home that afternoon. Then who is on the sofa?

Ed grabbed a broom and poked the snoring body with its handle until a groggy, startled student woke up.

"Who are you? Stop hitting me, I'm sleeping."

"Who am I? I live here! This is my house! Who are you?" Ed yelled. Betty recognized the poor child before things got nasty. It was the Johnson kid, who grew up three houses down the street. An honor student. After Ed chased him home, he found Betty looking at the sofa.

"He had an accident. We've really got to start locking the door."

"But we know it's Jackson who's here and not some stray lamb. We know he got off the plane because the Caldwells saw him at the airport when they picked up their Kirstin. He was waiting for his roommate to come through the baggage claim."

"His roommate flew in the baggage compartment?"

"They say it's better than coach. More leg room. And you never get bumped. Besides, he's from some country that's so poor, their president travels that way."

"And they say you never learn anything useful in college."

"No, they say *you* never learned anything useful in college; the rest of us learned a lot."

Just then there was a loud crash and the sound of swearing from upstairs. It sounded as if someone was hopping around on one foot. I heard a door slam shut. Millie and Dan smiled. "Maybe we'll see him for dinner," she said.

Don't Think with Your Mouth Full

I don't know if it's an iron-clad rule but I always heard it was considered impolite to talk about religion, politics, or money at the dinner table. It makes sense because we should enjoy eating together, not dread it. And it still leaves plenty of things to talk about—work, family, sports, pets, hobbies, and if all else fails, at least you can talk about the food.

"Mmmm, it's wonderful," I said to Libby, our hostess. "The best chicken I've had in a long time."

"I didn't know people still ate meat," said Cabernet from the far end of the table. "The mere thought of eating animal flesh makes me sick."

Cabernet, I found out later, had become a totally committed, radical vegan at one o'clock yesterday morning on a first date with her new boyfriend, Willoughby.

"I always heard Hitler was a vegetarian," said Don between bites. The sudden silence around the table made him realize that this factoid could be taken the wrong way. He quickly added, "So was George Bernard Shaw. And Julius Caesar and, oh, lots of famous people."

"I can hear the poor thing scream with every bite you take!" Cabernet snapped and took another swig of white wine. Libby was not offended.

"I don't think chickens scream. They cluck, don't they? Anyway, the guy at the store said it was cruelty-free, free-range chicken."

"You don't think cutting off its head, pulling out all its feathers and gutting it and then cooking it and cutting it up with a knife and a fork and sticking it in your mouth is cruel?" slurred Cabernet. "What if a chicken did that to you?"

"That's life at the bottom of the food chain," said Libby. "Don't you watch those nature shows? If we didn't eat chickens, foxes and coyotes would. We've all got to die of something."

"Nothing eats us," Cabernet said.

"Lots of things eat us," said Don. "Grizzly bears, sharks, all kinds of bacteria, lions, piranha . . ."

"I love what you've done with the asparagus," I interrupted trying to change the subject to something less contentious.

"I don't know why anyone would buy stuff that's not in season in our neck of the woods," said Willoughby. "This stuff probably came from Chile. The carbon footprint of flying a pound of fresh asparagus from there to here in the winter must be huge."

Cabernet gave him an adoring look as if he'd just slain a dragon for her. A gigantic, meat-eating dragon. Libby was starting to feel under-appreciated.

"Maybe," she said, "they put it on the same plane that brought you back from that vacation in Arizona."

At least we weren't talking about religion, politics or money. That can make people angry. This was more like it, fellowship among friends, breaking bread together in a spirit of . . .

"I think it's time we should go," said Cabernet.

"Oh, you have to taste the dessert. It's vegetarian, you can eat it, I promise it won't scream. It's a pound cake. A pound of sugar, a pound of butter, a pound of flour . . ."

The little color there was drained from Cabernet's face. "Sugar! Butter! Flour! Why don't you just pull out a gun and kill us?"

"I wasn't planning to but now I'll have to think about it," Libby said under her breath.

"You know, Hitler. . . ."

"Shut up!" we all yelled at Don.

"Anyone for coffee?" Libby asked.

"Is it organic, fair-wage coffee roasted locally by homeless people?" Willoughby asked.

"I'm sorry, I didn't mean to interrupt you, Don," Libby said. "What were you saying about Hitler?"

It got worse after that. Cabernet and Willoughby left in a wordless rush; Libby couldn't wait to see their backs. On the ride home Sue said, "Add food to the list of things you can't talk about at dinner."

From the Fat into the Fire

D on't worry, dear, the men of the family will be cooking the turkey this year, you can put your feet up and relax this holiday. All you have to do is make the mashed potatoes, the sweet potatoes, the vegetables, the pies, clean the house, and set the table; we'll do the rest.

HOW TO DEEP FAT FRY A TURKEY

INSTRUCTIONS

- Drink a few twelve-packs of Bud Light while the peanut oil heats up on the back patio.
- Have a few beers figuring out if the turkey should go in when the oil is boiling or wait until it starts to smoke.

- Have a few beers figuring out how many minutes per pound it should cook.
- Someone suggests defrosting the turkey. For 15 minutes.
- Gather round to lower the frozen bird into the boiling smoking oil.
- Watch closely as the 25-pound bird slips out of the chef's hands and belly flops into a bucket of boiling, smoking peanut oil near an open flame.
- Whoomp!
- Stomp out the flames on your burning friends while screaming "What's the number for 911?"
- While in the hospital waiting for skin grafts, make plans to trebuchet next year's turkey into boiling oil at a safe distance.

Martha Stewart's Evil Twin

QUICK AND EASY TURKEY
PREPARATION TIME, 10 SECONDS

1. Drive to Costco.
2. Buy a big, cooked and stuffed turkey.
3. Take it home.
4. Warm it up in the oven and put it on a platter.
5. Don't tell anyone the recipe.

QUICK AND EASY PUMPKIN PIE

1. Drive to the grocery store.
2. Buy some pies.
3. Buy some whipped cream.
4. Put the pies in your own pie pans.
5. Heat them up in the oven.

6. Put whipped cream in a bowl. Whip it around with a fork so it looks like you made it yourself.
7. Don't talk about the recipe.

QUICK AND EASY HORS D'OEUVRES

1. Go to the grocery store.
2. Buy some fancy-looking hors d'oeuvres.
3. Bring them home.
4. Put them on your own serving dishes.
5. Hide the boxes.
6. Don't talk about the recipe.

FANCY CONDIMENTS

1. Go to the grocery store.
2. Buy inexpensive, oddball pickles, olives and cheeses.
3. Put them on fancy trays.
4. Pretend you bought them at a Farmer's Market.

The Ghost of Christmas Parties Past

My friends and I gather for brunch three weeks before Christmas, before the deep crazy begins, knowing it will be our last get-together of the year. They all had stories of holiday downsizing.

"Two years ago we had the office party at a fancy nightclub. Last year it was in the executive conference room. This year it's going to be separate checks at an Olive Garden." Paul missed the open bar of years gone by. He missed the uniformed waiters circulating with trays of hors d'oeuvres and flutes of champagne. He missed the Christmas bonuses. But mostly he missed making other people do his job. Now, with the staff cuts, he had to do the work of all the people he used to manage.

Ellen works for a consulting firm across town. She wasn't happy, either. "Our party this year is going to be in the eighth floor cafeteria. No liquor. They're going with fruit punch. What person in their right mind will make a pass at me if they're sober? Which means I won't have anyone to blackmail next year and I don't think I can make it on my crappy salary alone. A drunken pass by a married executive was always good for a few days off or being able to come in late every now and then. It was part of my bonus package. No drunks, no bonuses."

"My company used to hire famous entertainers for the party every year," Dale said. "A few years ago it was Britney Spears. This year all they can afford is some has-been who can't get arrested on Saturday night."

"Who is it?"

"Britney Spears."

"We used to get ten paid days off and a free turkey. This year we got two days off and a can of store-brand cranberry sauce," said Ellen. "Maybe the fruit punch will ferment in some executive's stomach and he'll do something foolish."

"Maybe it's time to get back to the true meaning of the office party," Paul countered. "Isn't it the one time of year you can get drunk and bond with your cubicle mates?"

"At my office, we do that every Monday, Wednesday and Friday. Besides, half my cubicle mates are in India," Ellen said. "One of them wanted to know why we wear scary costumes and say 'Trick or Treat' at Christmas. I told them it was something we got from the Pilgrims. They don't even know the rest of the company gets Christmas Day off."

"Does your company make the Indians take English sounding names?" I asked.

"Are you kidding?" she said. "Sanjay and Lakshmi *are* English sounding names now. And the customers don't care what their names are anyway. They're happy just to yell at a human. Next year I'm afraid the only people at our Christmas party will be me and the woman who says, 'If you'd like to continue this phone call in English, press one.' I hear they're looking to get rid of her."

"That's the holiday spirit," said Dale, "My cousin got a pink slip in his bonus envelope last year."

"What did he do?"

"He sold fax machines. This recession killed his business."

"Yeah, that must have taken him by surprise," Paul said, "Maybe he can switch to selling portable typewriters. I hear they're flying off the shelves."

"I miss the good old days," said Ellen, putting on her coat.

"Then I'll have another drink and sexually harass you. It'll be just like the old days," said Paul.

"Sorry, I'll have to take a rain check. I was supposed to be at my second job an hour ago."

"What's your second job?"

"Holiday party planner."

What to Get the Man Who Has Everything

With oil close to one hundred dollars a barrel and Christmas right around the corner, gasoline may turn out to be this year's Tickle Me Elmo. The most popular "Santa" may be the person who shows up with a gift-wrapped, five-gallon jerry can of regular, not the guy with the latest iPod or the smallest cell phone. And gas makes a great present for everyone—granny or grandkid, boss or employee, rich or poor.

What do you get the person who has everything? Gas! What do you get that hard-to-shop-for person? Gas! What gift to give the host of the Christmas dinner? Candles? A bottle of wine? Homemade cookies? Flowers?

Why not five gallons of gas? (Just a note from personal experience: make sure your host doesn't put it near the open flame by the chafing dishes.)

No one returns gas the day after Christmas; you can give as much or as little as you want; you can do all your shopping in one place and at the last minute. Say you find out someone you didn't shop for will be at a Christmas party. On your way to the party you can stop and pick up some gas. What could be easier? It saves a lot of running around; it saves gas. Gas containers already come in Christmas red, but when oil hits two hundred dollars a barrel some time next year, I'm sure companies will start making "gift cans" with the appropriate decorations— birthday cans, anniversary cans, and graduation gas cans for the student. And remember, it's imported! Nothing says class like something from another country. And it's from the Holy Land. Not Jesus's Holy Land, but somebody's.

I was kind of surprised that this year's Neiman Marcus "Christmas Book" featured a million-and-a-half-dollar submarine instead of, say, your own personal backyard oil field and refinery. I'm sure the submarine is a swell gift, and certainly better than their cheesy $73,000 diamond-encrusted cell phone or their low-end $398 "Hobo" purse. If that's all you can afford for a purse, why bother? You probably don't have any money to put in it.

And after all, how often were you going to use the stupid submarine? And what's it going to run on? Nuclear power? Of course not. It'll need tons of that hundred-dollar-a-barrel oil. If only your spouse had been thoughtful enough to buy you your own personal refinery . . . Why, hardly a day would go by where you couldn't use that. And boy, wouldn't the neighbors be jealous! Well, there's always next Christmas.

A lot of people will say that petroleum is not a very romantic present. Sure, nothing says "I love you" like a crock pot or gift certificate to a tattoo parlor or that little hammer that lets you shatter the window when you're trapped under water in your car, but with a little dressing up, gas can be as romantic as any of those.

We have a saying around our house, "Little gifts come in small packages," and no one wants a little gift. When you give someone a five-gallon container full of gas properly wrapped—they know they've been gifted. Perhaps it's the world's largest diamond, they will think. Or a wall safe. Or a lifetime supply of hair gel. And when they shake it, few people can guess what's inside. Unless you've forgotten to screw on the cap all the way. (Let me tell you, that is a hard smell to get out of a sofa, no matter what you do.)

So why not think outside the gift box this Christmas and think inside the gas container? The next time you're at the pump, instead of thinking how much money you're pumping out of your bank account and into your car, you'll think of all the joy you've brought to your friends and family this holiday season. And your friends at OPEC.

New Year's Predictions

I just got my crystal ball back from the cleaners and have looked deep into the coming year. While not every prediction I made last year came true (Elvis was not discovered working at a Dairy Queen outside Biloxi), I feel much more confident this year. I'm hoping to break 95 percent accuracy for the first time. I predict:

That the stock market will go up. Then down. Then up. Then down. It will repeat this roughly 52 times.

Several sports figures will be caught doing something illegal, immoral, or fattening. They will be soundly denounced by alcoholic sports reporters who cheat on their wives and bet on sporting events.

Several world-famous actors and actresses will go through messy divorces. It will have absolutely no effect on anybody's life outside of their immediate families and friends. We will get tired of hearing about it three months before *Entertainment Tonight* does.

Scientists will discover a miracle cure for an illness you don't have.

Scientist will discover a cure for that four-hour-long erection, but no one will buy it.

Something you have eaten your whole life will be found to cause cancer in rats. Twenty years from now they will discover that all rats die of cancer.

Tens of thousands of people will ring in the New Year in Times Square. None of them will be from New York City.

Several politicians will make racist or sexist remarks for which they will have to apologize. They will be the same politicians that had to apologize last year.

A crusading preacher will be caught with his pants down or his hand in the collection basket. Or vice versa. Or both.

Several celebrities will enter rehab. They couldn't deal with the pressure of having so much money.

Something real will happen on a reality show. It may not happen this year, or next year, but one day, it will happen.

People who live in the flood plains will get flooded. They will be shocked. Out-of-control fires will burn down homes in California. The owners will be shocked. A tornado will rip through a trailer park. Survivors will be shocked.

Forecasters will predict the "Storm of the Century" five times this year. Four of them won't be very bad and you'll wonder what all the fuss was about.

Your favorite team will have another disappointing year. Everybody will know exactly what's wrong with the team except the rich guy who owns it.

Someone close to you will marry the wrong person. You will try to talk them out of it. They will stop speaking to you. Even after the divorce.

Someone close to you will get divorced. You will say you never liked the spouse. The couple will get back together. They will stop speaking to you.

Someone will become famous for doing something stupid.

Someone will become famous for doing something smart.

There will be a new eat-all-you-want-and-never-feel-hungry diet craze that will consist of an odd combination of foods and rituals. Something like "Eat all the spaghetti you want after 10 P.M. No sauce of any kind. For breakfast, all the anchovies you can eat in five minutes. No coffee. Watch the pounds melt away."

No matter how much money you have, you will wish you had more.

You will break all of your New Year's resolutions.

Tree Strikes and You're Out

We took down our Christmas tree today, a few weeks after the holiday, packed up all the lights, put away all the silver balls. We could have done it sooner, but it smells nice and the lights are cheery on these short winter days, so we left it up until the middle of January.

We may hang on to our tree too long, but others don't hang on to them long enough. I started seeing forlorn, empty Christmas trees, still sprouting tinsel and popcorn strings, on the curbsides of town the day after Christmas. They looked perfectly green, perfectly shaped, kicked out of the house before their time. What was the big rush? Do parents think their children will expect to find more presents under the tree each day it stays in the house?

On the other hand, we know people who wait way too long. One woman we know won't take her tree down until April. It seems odd to go to her house on St. Patrick's Day to eat her yearly corned beef and cabbage dinner and find a fully decorated Christmas tree in her living room, the lights blazing, surrounded by a living carpet of fifty or so poinsettias; but where's the harm in that?

Unfortunately her husband is not as much of a fan of Christmas as she is. Josephina is a perfectionist when it comes to her tree. She always goes to the same "cut your own" place an hour away and she spends hours poking and judging and measuring to get just the right tree. It has to be a Fraser Fir. It has to be seven feet, three inches tall. She's a tiny woman so she brings a stepladder and a measuring tape and a saw with her. Over the years she has built up quite a little tree-cutting kit.

Her husband Ralph used to go with her with all the enthusiasm of a man who has been asked to carry his wife's purse while she digs through fabric remnants. The hours away from the television set nearly killed him. He could be home watching The Game if only she could be like a normal person and buy any old tree.

"Who is going to know the difference? It's a dumb old pine tree, for God's sake. And you're going to decorate it within an inch of its life so no one will even know if it's a pine or a spruce or a maple tree. I'm freezing—let's hurry it up and cut down a tree already?"

But Josephina would know. Everything in her house is just so; she vacuums so often it's a wonder the color hasn't been sucked out of the carpets.

When they finally get the tree home there will be a day-long shouting match over how to get it in the tree stand. It has been going on like this for years, but finally even Josephina couldn't stand it any longer. She started taking other people with her to buy the tree instead of Ralph.

Josephina liked to get her tree a month before Christmas because it would take her almost a week to get all the Christmas decorations out of the attic and decorate it.

This year it was Sue's turn to go with Josephina to cut down her tree. I expected her to be gone all day but Sue got back in only three hours.

"The one she wanted was practically in front of the place where we parked," Sue said. "She loved the shape;

she got out her step ladder and measuring tape and it was the right height and we cut it down and brought it home. I don't think I've ever seen her so happy in my life."

By chance, the very next day I drove past Ralph and Josephina's house. There was a forlorn, empty tree lying out by the curbside that looked a lot like a seven-foot-three-inch tall Fraser Fir. I knew right away that Ralph had once again cut too much off the bottom to fit it in the tree stand and that the tree was now seven foot two or seven foot one and that they must have had the screaming match to end all screaming matches, and that this poor tree was the cause of it all.

How different the holiday might have been if she had spent as much time looking for the perfect husband as she had for the perfect tree.

The Pre-Mid-Winter Break

Welcome back, class. I hope you all completed your Pre-Mid-Winter Break reading assignments in Classical Literature, *The Hunger Games* and *Harry Potter*. We'll be discussing those and the other classics like *Twilight* this semester. Don't forget, we have to get through *Chicken Soup for Teens* before the fourteen-day Mid-Winter Break which starts next Thursday.

Those of you who had Mr. Grunion for remedial addition last semester should know he had an exciting Pre-Mid-Winter Break. I suppose the easiest way to explain it is that he's Miss Grunion now, and in addition to teaching math, she will be coaching the girl's softball team. Go Redheads! As you know, the Redheads had a one-and-fourteen season last year and Miss Grunion thinks they're capable of doing even more. At least twice as well, she promises. Still, they did capture their third "Courage to Show Up" Cup which is displayed in the trophy case in the main hall. Two more of those and we will have more of them than any other high school in the state.

The school board has made a few rule changes, so listen up. All tattoos must be tasteful and PG-13. No swear words without a parent or guardian's permission, especially on the fingers. There will be a limit of three piercings per face, excluding the ears. That is, you could have one eyebrow, one lip and one nose pierced, or two eyebrows and one nose, but you can't have two eyebrows, a nose and a lip. Is that understood?

It's harsh, but these rules are for your own protection. We had several painful and ugly accidents last year and no one wants a repeat of that. I think that picture of Billy Chambers stuck to the tennis court fence will haunt me for the rest of my life. They say his nose reattachment went well, but he still hasn't been able to return to class.

As you all know, thongs must be worn "inside" your clothes. What you do at home is your own business but here at school we have standards. There will be no online shopping allowed this year during school hours. Those iPads are for studying, people, not shopping. And don't bother to try. We've worked out a deal with FedEx, they will no longer deliver packages to this school except to teachers and administrators. Is that clear?

Anyone violating these rules will be sent to a school that is even more expensive than this one. Remember, five or six strikes and you're out. Or you will at least be spoken to, so watch it.

We have installed video games in the detention hall, but unlike last year, these games are *two* years old instead of one! And we didn't resurface the pool table. So, if that doesn't keep you on your best behavior, I don't know what will.

Between the Post-Mid-Winter Holiday and the Pre-Mid-Winter Rest we've added a teacher's conference, so there are only nineteen school days between December 15th and April 5th and we will have to cram in a lot of work.

There has been a change in the History curriculum; we'll be studying the second season of *Gossip Girl* this year, not the first year as it says in your printed class schedule. In the two weeks between the Pre-Summer Student-Stress-Relief Break and the April 10th Summer Orientation break we will be covering *That 70s Show* so if you haven't started watching that, you'd better get started. There will be a quiz on the fashions of the 70s as well as the decor. Remember, "Those who don't watch TV are doomed to watch repeats."

Sit down, Mr. Wilson. The mid-morning snack bell hasn't rung yet. Starbucks will still be in the cafeteria when the bell rings. Which reminds me, those of you who have signed up for "Cell Phone Plan Management," would you please raise your hands? That's not many. I know it's the toughest course we offer, but you really should think about taking it. It will stretch your minds and save you money. There's the bell. Remember, you've only got an hour snack this year, so try not to be late for your next class.

Black Friday Redux

The Friday after Thanksgiving is the biggest shopping day of the year. What have people got to buy that is so important that it can't wait until Saturday? Or next Tuesday? Or two weeks from now? Or until, say, late afternoon of Christmas Eve, the way I do? I save hours of shopping because all the good stuff is gone and there aren't nearly so many choices to make. What's left is stuff nobody really wants or the stuff that's really expensive.

Oh, there are good deals on things on Black Friday, but you know when there are really good deals on things? A few weeks *after* Christmas. That's when a gift certificate, or better yet, cash, would come in handy. A lot of people think giving cash is tacky. None of those people are teenagers. And let's say two or three people give you cash, then you can combine it to buy whatever you like, instead of that crappy hand-knit sweater Aunt Eileen gave you. How can you return that? I'll have to put it on eBay to get any money out of it. I mean "you'll" have to put it on eBay. People say it's the thought that counts. Here's a thought—give me cash. There's no line to buy cash on Black Friday. Just go to any ATM machine. And they usually have the newest bills. Or don't even leave the house, just write a check. Besides, cash money is one of the few things we still make in this country. So giving money isn't just smart, it's patriotic.

Some stores are going to open at 5 A.M. the day after Thanksgiving. If you're going shopping at 5 A.M., what time do you get up? 4 A.M.? At 4 A.M. on Black Friday I am going to be under the covers dreaming of sugar plum fairies. Well, maybe not, since I haven't the foggiest idea of what a sugar plum fairy is. Are they the ones that leave cash under your pillow or are they more like Tinker Bell?

As much as I would love to spend my day off looking for a parking space in a crowded parking lot, I'm going to skip all the Black Friday festivities—the fist fights, the screaming babies, the screaming adults, catching whatever killer flu is going around this holiday season, the fender benders, the crowded food courts, the long lines at the wrapping desks and the cash registers. One woman told me she does it so she's sure the stores won't run out of the gifts she "needs" to get. I wonder who is out getting her the gift she will need this Christmas—a second job to pay for all the gifts she bought on Black Friday.

The Big Shop of Horrors

A month before Christmas, in the middle of hunting season, a gigantic new store for outdoorsmen opened near us and my deer-hunting brother-in-law Dave took me along for a quick gift-buying trip. Who doesn't want a nice turkey caller this holiday? Or a pair of waders? Or a bottle of deer urine? Now you can get all three under one giant roof.

The store looks like one of those giant rustic hotels you see in national parks. It is made out of immense peeled logs, sixty or seventy feet long, as thick around as one of the prissily clean, brand-spanking-new pick-up trucks in the parking lot. Men won't clean the bathroom, they won't wash a dish, but God forbid there's a speck of dirt on their pick-up. Someone will pay. The building almost screams "Teddy Roosevelt Slept Here" except for the fact that it was obviously built yesterday. The testosterone is still wet.

Massive, twelve-point deer heads hang along either side of the main aisle which leads to a forty foot-tall man-made mountain decorated with taxidermied animals in the center of the store. It is like Noah's Ark in reverse; they've killed two of everything, from chipmunks to grizzly bears, from big-horned sheep to giant sloths. The only thing it lacks is a Sasquatch.

"Why is it that being stuffed and mounted is good enough for a grizzly, but not good enough for, say, Grandpa?" I asked Dave. "Why did we spring for a head-stone, when for the same price we could have had him stuffed and put in the den? I think he'd go as well with our décor as any stuffed elk or mountain goat." Dave said nothing. Like his sister, he often ignores me.

Past Mounted Mountain on the right is the Cold and Wet Department—an endless variety of canoes, kayaks, fishing rods, tackle, and flies. On the left is Death Valley—rifles, shotguns, bows, arrows, deer stands. In between the two departments is everything the camper could desire—camp stoves, lightweight pots, flashlights, bug spray, tents, sleeping bags. If it's not in this store, it doesn't exist. An outdoor lover could drop a paycheck in here faster than you can say, "Hand me that brand new snake bite kit."

It is sooo manly that even the underwear they sell has a camouflage pattern on it. I saw a guy walk by pushing two toddlers in a camouflage stroller. This is so far past my macho comfort level it's off the chart. The only thing I have ever stalked is a dust bunny. And it got away. It's not like I'm Truman Capote, but I am an indoorsman. To me, game is something you play, not something you shoot.

As we walked around, I spotted a rack of fleece jackets with a nylon shell on the outside for nineteen dollars apiece. I wear those synthetic fleece things around the house all the time because, unlike sweaters, they have pockets and you can just toss them in the wash.

For nineteen dollars, these things are a steal. So I take off my jacket and slip one off the hanger. Just as I stick my arm into the sleeve, a salesman rushes up to me. Just as he gets to me, there is one of those strange, rare moments when everything in the store goes quiet for half a second. The cash registers stop beeping, the music track is in between songs, all the customers seem to be taking one deep breath at the same moment. You could hear him from the front of the store to the back as he said in a megaphone-like voice, "Sir, those are women's jackets!" I guess I should have known from the camouflage panty hose that I was in the Women's Department but I honestly didn't see them. They blended in too well with the camouflage bras and camouflage thongs.

To the store's credit, they didn't ask me to leave. It was Dave who suggested I might be more comfortable waiting for him back in the truck.

New New Year's Resolutions Solution

I'm sick of making New Year's resolutions only to break them a few weeks later. Well, a few days later. OK, a few hours later. What I mean to say is a few minutes later. Not only that, I usually end up doing the opposite of what I resolve to do. If I resolve to lose weight, I gain it. If I resolve to exercise more, I exercise less. One year I resolved to quit smoking. Not only didn't I quit, I made three people who didn't smoke, start. So this year I had a brainstorm. I resolve to do the opposite of what I should do and see how that works.

One: I resolve to watch more television. I saw a newspaper story the other day that said the average viewer watches five hours of television a day. "Finally," I thought, "I'm above average." I think, if I put my mind to it, I could watch nine or ten hours of television a day. I might have to get up earlier, but that's the thing about New Year's resolutions. If they were easy, everybody would make them.

Two: I resolve to gain more weight. This one is going to be tough. Where will I ever find enough fattening, greasy, sugar-loaded food to do that? It's not like you can just find that kind of stuff on the side of the road. You really have to dig. We can put a man on the moon but we can't make a little pill that will make us fat? No, instead we have to spend hours and hours eating. Of course to meet my first resolution of watching more TV I will have to multitask. Eat and watch television at the same time.

Three: I resolve to spend less time exercising. This will be the first one I break. Since I spend no time exercising now, simply typing these words may be the most strenuous thing I did last year.

Memo to me: Buy one of those programs where you talk to the computer and it types for you.

Four: Spend more time on the internet. A lot of people wonder if being on the internet so much is a good thing for society. Sure, it's broken up a few hundred thousand marriages, but thanks to internet dating, it's now easier than ever for those people to meet, marry, and divorce new people.

The internet lets me use my time more productively. I used to spend a lot of time with my family but now I spend most of my time researching my family tree. My dead relatives are so much less annoying than my live ones. Plus you learn about history when you learn about your family. Some people can trace their families back to the *Mayflower*. I can trace my family back to a Carnival Cruise in 1976. It turns out that unlike most of the Irish we didn't come to America because of the famine. We came because we were asked to leave.

Five: Spend more time on the cell phone. I'm so ashamed. I don't know how to text. I can never remember my cell phone number. When someone leaves me a message I have to dig out the manual to find out how to hear it. I barely use it. You'd think I would have a lot of things to say on a cell phone but if I average a phone call a week, I'd be surprised. Yet I know fifteen-year-old kids in high school who make and receive more phone calls in a day than the CEOs of Fortune 500 companies. There are kids in college that field more phone calls than George Clooney's agent. How did I ever get through high school without a cell phone? I feel like a cell phone slacker. This year I plan to start calling people up even though I have nothing to say to them and nothing's really changed since I talked to them ten minutes ago. Because all I did was watch TV, eat and fool around on the internet. Unless, as usual, I break all my resolutions.

Santa's Lament

Do you ever wonder what I do on the 364 days when I'm not delivering toys? Mostly, I try to figure out what kids will want next Christmas. It's hard; kids are so picky. Why do they think I come by in the middle of the night? Because they're asleep, that's why. I don't have to listen to their whining if they didn't get exactly what they wanted. So what if it's the wrong color? It's a dump truck. Now, if it were a fire engine. . . .

Don't get me wrong, I'm not complaining about the job. I get to pick my own hours and I'm my own boss. Besides, what else would I do at my age? Become a barista at Starbucks? A personal trainer? A life coach? But like any other job, it has its problems. Maybe you heard about the flooding at my place this past summer? No ice at the North

121

Pole for the first time in, like, oh yeah, *history!* Thanks, guys. I've had to move my whole operation to the South Pole just to be safe. It's horrible. I keep tripping over those *March of the Penguins* people filming Part Two, but the North Pole will still be my mail drop for the next several years until I can send out all the change of address forms. To make up the cost of the move, every present I deliver for the next fifty years will say "Some Assembly Required."

Then the elves threatened to go on strike until I coughed up for health insurance and a shorter work week. Who do they think I am? Google? Who do they think is going to pay for that? The tooth fairy? We had her over for dinner last week and trust me, she's got her own problems. You leave a kid a quarter for a tooth nowadays and they stop believing in you. They want two bucks, minimum. She's going through cash faster than a Presidential candidate. Her expenses have gone through the roof. Plus, she's dating a real creep. Somebody she met online.

I'm telling you all this because I want you to know that when Santa's got a problem, you've got a problem. And here it is: I base the presents I buy this year on what was hot last year. Sure, it's not an exact science, but I pretty much know that if every kid wanted Guitar Hero last year, I'm going to need a lot of them this year, too. Sure, every now and then some Tickle Me Elmo or Cabbage Patch fad comes along that I didn't see coming, but by and large I get it right.

Last year I couldn't believe what children wanted for Christmas. One nine-year-old asked me for an AmEx Platinum Card, a fifty-inch plasma HDTV for her room, a week-long spa vacation, a Justin Bieber performance in her house for her and her three best friends, a fake ID that said she was eleven, *and a pony*. If I didn't get it for her, her parents would. So I loaded up on expensive stuff for this Christmas. Video games, iPods, cameras, Blu-ray players—you name it, I got warehouses full of it at the South Pole just waiting for the asking. So what happens? I got my first "Dear Santa" letter of the year two weeks ago. The kid doesn't want anything for herself, she wants me to give her dad a job. That, I ain't got. The next one says, "Dear Santa, My mom says the way things are going, we won't have a roof over our heads. Could you get us a roof? Thanks, Tracy."

I'm sorry, but a roof is not a toy. Based on last year's statistics, she's scheduled to get a Hannah Montana backpack. What am I going to do with all the iPhones and Wii games? After this Christmas I'll be lucky to get any mail at all. The kids can't afford stamps.